A SOLDIERS JOURNEY

Shaun

Lovely to meet you and many thanks for your support. Enjoy

*[signature]*

THE BUSINESS BATTLEFIELD

First published in the United Kingdom in 2017

Copyright © Nick Wilson 2017

The moral right of the author has been asserted.
All rights reserved.

No part of this publication may be reproduced, stored in a retrieval system, or transmitted, in any form or by any means, without the prior permission in writing of the author, nor be otherwise circulated in any form of binding or cover other than that in which it is published and without a similar condition including this condition being imposed on the subsequent purchaser.

ISBN

Cover design by

www.rorcreative.com

# Dedicated to...

This book is dedicated to all those I served with over the years, those I served under and those to who, I was an unknown.
To those who have served and laid down their lives, to those who feel the pain and a fear, of a lifetime alone.

To Madison and Emily, my beautiful girls, of who I have missed more than I can abide. The strength I gain, to keep up the fight, comes from the thought of you both and the love I feel inside. I have not been there for you, not a great Father or friend. I dedicate this book to you, offering it as a sign, of how far I have come and the lengths I will go, until I prove once more, how much I love you so – I LOVE YOU.

# Acknowledgments

There are so many individuals who have supported me over the years and without whom, I have no doubt, I would not be here right now, let alone writing a book. For that, I sincerely thank you all.

A special mention goes to: Batch, such belief, trust and respect that goes beyond words and could never be repaid. Darren, my first Civvie, true and trusted friend, who is also a wonderful Photographer. Rory, with the patience of a saint, genuine heart and soul, creating the Graphic Design magic that you do. Ben, the words of wisdom, advice and support, that keep me reigned in and forever in focus.

# CONTENTS

    Acknowledgments

    Introduction      Pg 7

1. Military Skills in Business      Pg 13
2. Courage      Pg 21
3. Discipline      Pg 29
4. Respect      Pg 37
5. Integrity      Pg 45
6. Loyalty      Pg 51
7. Selfless Commitment      Pg 57
8. Summary      Pg 65
9. About Nick      Pg 71

# Introduction

On 12 December 2012, I was officially Discharged from the British Army after some 14 years service. Those years had seen me deploy on several Operational Tours around the globe including: Northern Ireland, Kosovo, Iraq and Afghanistan.

I was fully fit when I joined, yet on my discharge – a result of government redundancies – I had chronic spinal pain with several prolapsed discs and (as I was to find out) Post Traumatic Stress Disorder – PTSD – dating back to Kosovo in 2001. In January 2015, these issues led to my being officially classed as "Disabled".

I felt prepared for leaving the Army and attended the Career Transition Workshop, now being provided by the Career Transition Partnership. I felt the workshop was a waste of time for me personally due to the life experiences I had from before joining the Army. Learning how to be in an interview scenario and the varying ways of writing a CV just did not seem relevant. Being shown how our skills transfer across and what jobs, aside from being a truck driver, were realistically available was more what I had hoped for.

Things have improved in the four years since my leaving; but there are still many reports of people slipping through the cracks, and of the Career Transition Partnership – CTP – simply being overwhelmed by the approximately 16,000 service personnel who leave annually.

As time would demonstrate, with no real understanding of my own skills and abilities, or how transferrable they might be, the transition was going to test me as an individual. I was most certainly not ready for the range of emotions, frustrations, difficulties and challenges that resulted from this transition. I still today find various elements of life and business a challenge.

Although I had done the same as many and completed my Close Protection Operator – CPO – Course to gain that "Golden ticket" otherwise known as the Close Protection SIA badge, which apparently could earn you up to £500 per day (yeah, right!) there were no openings in that field. Some were lucky, but the industry was saturated with ex-Forces personnel; so I chose another path, turning my skills to something different, and managed to get a job as a chauffeur to keep me going whilst I went through the "transition" that I knew had to be faced at some point.

After a few months and various disagreements with a member of management, I was asked to move on. Right there was my introduction to the reality of business and political correctness in civilian life. The first lesson was learned and duly noted. I did not have a clue what else to do at this point, so I went back to catering for a little while, working as an events manager. I had worked in this industry prior to joining the Army.

Then it hit me, why not take the jump and start my own chauffeur company? At the time I had very little money and my credit score was poor but I was lucky enough to meet someone who was ex Navy (he later became a good friend) who offered me use of his Jaguar XJL to use as my first chauffeur car.

In a matter of weeks I went from being an Events Manager to starting my own business, being self-employed for the first time in my life. I launched Premier Platinum, or – as it would become known – Purely Platinum.

My personal experience was that there was little support from outside agencies and so lesson two was learned: although there is support out there (and more so now four years on) it can be confusing and emotionally tiring searching and sorting through the resources to find the ones relevant to you.

"Self Help" is key, so get used to it and do not waste your time waiting for others to come to your aid or arguing the point that someone should be doing something about it. You will waste invaluable time and energy, which can be used more productively in planning your future, gaining clarity on your specific goals and, most importantly, identifying the skills you have that can be transferred from the military in order to gain employment or structure your new business.

I made a promise to myself when I first started in business, that I would stay true to who I was. I would stand by the Army's values and standards, which I had lived by for my entire military career. I would use the business to help others, continuing on the charity work that I had worked so hard at during my Army life, raising some £50k+ over the years.

That sounds easy enough, right? It's not like I was trying to save the world, become a millionaire or even treat anyone better than a normal human being. In fact this experience has been the hardest thing I have known! Save for the death and destruction to people's lives, there were times where I would have rather been back on Tour in Kosovo, Iraq or even Afghanistan. At least I could have got a sun tan whilst going through all the shit; but more seriously, the fact that I could always rely on my fellow Services brothers and sisters surrounding me was the saving grace that kept me sane through those years of service.

It took me four years of heartache, upset, disappointment and absolute dumbfoundness before I finally came to the realisation – and most importantly acceptance – that the business world simply does not play by the same rules we do in the military. Life can be so very different. I thought I was ready for that: after all it is "Civvie Street", of course it will be different! But it can be the little things that take you by surprise, frustrate the hell out of you and leave you feeling very confused.

Values and standards are simply not held in the same high regard by everyone in business as they are in the Military. This fact can actually be reframed and used to your advantage in business, but for me, this does not make up for the lack of respect, integrity and/or loyalty. That cuts deep after years of being able to rely on them and living by them.

A prime example of this happened towards the end of 2016 – whilst I was still writing this book, in fact. It came from someone I thought I could trust, someone I thought of as a colleague, friend, hell, even a brother, with their being a fellow veteran! I cannot go into details, but it has left me in no doubt whatsoever that your "six" is not covered by even your closest ally, friend or Forces brother/sister in the business world.

It cut so very deep, I was shocked and in pain. This just doesn't happen where we come from, how the hell has it come to the point where even veterans fail to look out for one another at a time when it is all the more important and the "enemy", so to speak, is everywhere?

One word.

Money!

My key point in all this is that the rules we're used to don't apply. Regardless of whether someone is a fellow veteran and supposed trusted brother, be wary, carry out due diligence and do not be so trusting until they have proven themselves. Even then, learn that business and money is one thing, a true friendship away from all that is something totally different.

I appreciate that not everyone in the business world is like this. I can personally attest to the fact that there are good people out there, after the help and support I have received over the years. We are all individuals after all; but still it is a lot different than we are used to and it takes a lot of work towards acceptance before you get used to it. If you ever do!

That being said, however, it is clear that the respect I earned, the reputation and successful growth of my business, were greatly contributed to by my identifying, understanding and transferring all the skills learned in the Military and relating the relevant skills where required. As I said earlier, the lack of guaranteed values and standards within the business world means that these set us apart. By simply continuing to have self-belief and demonstrating the values and standards learned in the Armed Forces, you will be held in high regard, respected and ultimately, successful.

You are highly trained, highly motivated, with a breadth and depth of life experiences that few can emulate. You have more worth in business and to the UK economy – whether employed or self-employed – than you might realise.

Fully understanding, appreciating and accepting this proved to be a turning point in my life, a huge lesson learned; and one that will positively affect my future. It's a lesson I will be forever grateful for and one that I hope will provide reassurance, assistance and confidence to you, my Forces brother/sister, as you forge a new life for yourself, a life that I pray holds peace and every happiness for you.

Thank you for your service, your dedication to this country and your sacrifice. You face a different battle now, fighting on a different type of Battlefield.

# Military Skills In Business

*"Many veterans and reservists continue to be stereotyped or employers fail to recognise the transferable skills they've acquired during their service careers, such as communication skills, leadership, teamwork, social perceptiveness, flexibility, creative problem-solving, judgement and decision-making. As a consequence, a high proportion of veterans work in low paid, routine jobs or choose instead to enter the skilled trades, employed as builders, plumbers, electricians and technicians, where the military's vocational training is more easily translated"* - **Veterans Work, Recognising the potential of ex-service personnel, Deloitte Report, Nov 2016.**

I was always told that my military skills would be of use in "Civvie Street" and the business world, but it took me four years in business before I successfully identified them and realised just how invaluable they are. As we all know, hindsight is a wonderful thing. If only there had been someone around back then to take the time to go over everything with me, talk things through and explain even just the basics. If there had been I would be in a very different position right now.

I am where I am, however, and having thought things through whilst writing this book, I would not change any of it. All the challenges faced, ups/downs, happy/sad times, good/bad times, they are all experiences that have made me who I am today and put me in a position where I can now help others by reframing all these experiences and passing them forward.

Military trades and the more basic, key transferable skills, are held in such high regard within business, although we Forces personnel do not always identify this straight away. Often it needs to be pointed out to us, and this may not happen till some while after discharge. On the whole, this is because a lot of what we all do on a daily basis as Service personnel is just simple, every day, basic routine – it's assumed, and we don't realise the rest of the world doesn't share it.

Turning up for "Parade" five minutes before it is due to start; the five minutes before the parade time – the constant "Hurry up and wait" mentality; daily inspections of your rooms and uniform; or sweeping the hangar and/or sweeping leaves outside on a breezy autumn day in the rain, because you were told to! It is easy to see how these things could be construed as pointless, not something to be communicated to a possible employer. On the face of it, that's true. Reworded, however, they translate into essential skills in the workplace: punctuality, discipline, smart appearance, ability to work unaided, ability to follow instructions.

If you Google the top ten skills that an employer might look for from an employee in business, it will return something along the lines of the following;

1. Time management
2. Communication
3. Teamwork
4. Problem solving
5. Organisational skills
6. Discipline
7. Values and Ethics
8. Ability to work under pressure
9. Motivation
10. Leadership and Management

Are you starting to see the pattern here? Of course you are! And your mind is also now starting to think of other things you have done which could be transferred across. Just think of all those seemingly pointless command tasks with oil drums, a plank of wood and some rope. How many times have we all done them throughout our careers? And yes, businesses actually pay handsomely for these skills in the work force, especially team leaders, line managers and management.

I cannot stress to you enough just how invaluable the skills, experiences and training you have gained over the years really are. That being said, many employers simply do not understand how many of these skills are transferable to their specific industry. They will also be looking for vocational training – as a plumber, for example.

The key to your being successful in gaining employment or

becoming self-employed, within a field where you would like to then forge a long lasting career, is having a clear understanding of your skills, experience and training, and how they transfer across into that industry. Then you need to relate them to a specific business in a way that communicates how they meet the requirements of that business.

*"There is a persistent lack of understanding of the key skills that veterans possess: for example, only 66 percent of medium and large organisations perceive veterans as having good communication skills, whereas this is a key strength highlighted by those organisations that have actually employed them. Veterans are disproportionately more likely than non-veterans to be employed in occupations where these skills are not as important, for instance as drivers of heavy-goods vehicles, security guards or metal-working production and maintenance fitters"* - **Veterans Work, Deloiite Report.**

The trade skills you possess are classed as "hard" skills; then you also have "soft" skills, such as leadership, communication and organisation.

Once you have an understanding of the skills you have, you will also require a clear understanding of what the organisation you are looking to join needs. Look past the hard skills and also identify the soft skills that would be of importance to them. When you have identified these and are able to relate your own skills to those required by an organisation, and demonstrate how they can be applied, you will be in a more commanding position as you enter into the business world – whether that is as an employee or self-employed.

I had made no plans when I first started out, and I didn't know any of the above. If I am honest, I didn't know what the hell I was doing. I had always been a bit 0 - 100mph, all or nothing, but this was to a totally different level. I strapped those lead boots to my feet and launched myself off the cliff, thinking I would figure things out as I went along. My first couple of years in business I was running around like a headless chicken, thrashing about like a bull in a china shop. I was the full range of animals, a one-stop zoo, with a feeling that I had to prove my worth to everyone.

I had an entrepreneurial desire to build a company that would grow, provide security for my children, employment for veterans, remove the stigma surrounding PTSD and prove my worth. I wanted to become a success and ……….. hide the fact I actually had a problem with my own PTSD.

I had the best of intentions, however this is not always enough. "Having the best intentions" was in some cases a righteous reason/excuse for the actions I took and my responses to the situations that arose. The point is that I made mistakes, in some cases pointless mistakes, and I ended up ruining relationships, making empty promises and costing the business money, all out of ignorance and naivety. So why was that?

There was no real plan, no structure or understanding of myself, my skills and how transferable they were to my business. I felt that I had to provide immediate results in order to prove my worth to those around me; and whilst I thought I was succeeding, what my business associates saw was the mobile zoo!

Don't be a "mobile zoo". Have a serious think about your own set of hard and soft skills, your values, what beliefs you have in yourself and have a specific, detailed plan with clearly defined goals. Remain flexible, have several plans, several CVs, carry out your due diligence, don't be afraid to ask questions and really carry out detailed research into your chosen areas.

Sound familiar? You see, things in business are very similar to how we conduct tasks and missions in the military. Just tone down the Forces terminology, identify, relate and transfer, and you will be amazed at the level of performance which can be achieved.

Once you have identified those hard and soft skills within you, it is then imperative that you understand how the components of your average professional individual are arranged or "Modelled" – i.e.: purpose, performance and process, underpinned by self-belief, personal values and standards. The structure of your average business is also based on a "Model" and this is: vision, mission, strategy, underpinned by the professional values and standards of the company.

Your ability to understand, relate and transfer yourself to the specific industries in which you may be looking for employment or starting a business will be the measure of your success.

Whilst there is much progress being made with various large global and UK companies, including some well-known brands, there is still so much more to be done, so many stigmas to be removed and industries to be educated about the value ex-Forces personnel can bring. As I mentioned previously, self-help and proactivity are key to ensuring that any transition into employment is as smooth as possible. The importance of having several well thought out and researched plans cannot be over emphasized.

For me, in addition to the importance of understanding the hard and soft skills you possess, it is just as important to understand yourself and your own set of beliefs, values and standards. I adopted the values and standards of the Armed Forces or courage, discipline, respect for others, integrity, loyalty and selfless commitment - CDRILS as we all know them – and embedded them as an integral part of my business ethos.

My company was built around them and I am convinced that one of the key reasons for its success over such a short space of time was my standing by this ethos. I continue to stand by it now, as I set out on my new journey.

Beliefs came later. Understanding my beliefs is a new addition to my life and one that takes pride of place next to values and standards. They are closely linked: if you have no belief in who you are, what you are doing and the values you stand by, then quite simply ………….. why would you do anything at all?

## Exercise: identifying your skills

What Skills do you have?

Hard Skills –

Soft Skills –

# Courage

**Oxford Dictionary definition -** *The ability to do something that frightens one.*

**Operational Definition -** *Soldiering has always demanded physical courage, to knowingly go into harm's way on behalf of the nation. Physical courage is required to risk life, take life, show restraint, endure hardships and focus on the task; soldiers depend on each other for it. Equally important is moral courage, the strength and confidence to do what is right, even when it may be unpopular and to insist on maintaining the highest standards of behavior and decency. This earns respect and fosters trust.*

Whilst you will appreciate the true definition of courage within the military, particularly whilst on the battlefield, this is more relating to physical courage. What about moral courage? And how do both transfer into business? Why should they?

Having courage to do the right thing in business is an incredibly difficult value to uphold at times. Everything in the business world revolves around money. Yes, business also consists of building a good reputation, rapport, reliability and professionalism, however business exists to make money. Even charities are in some sense businesses as they require to make money to operate. Ultimately money is the driver and money can be evil.

With this in mind, making a decision which might make or lose your company money, based on doing the right thing, takes incredible courage. The alternative is that you succumb to the pressure and fail to have the courage to make that right decision.

Courage is also the centerpiece of leadership and values-based leadership is highly regarded and highly successful in the corporate world. Courage is not only a necessary core component of effective leadership, it is the requisite platform on which other important tenets of leadership are built. As such, it is not something to simply bring forward and exercise at opportune times – it must be practiced day in and day out, by leaders at all levels, whether managers or part of the general workforce.

It takes great courage to stand up to your boss should they be doing something wrong or to admit it if you have made a mistake; it takes great courage to stand up for what you believe in if those around you do not agree. It takes great courage for a veteran to leave their Armed Forces family and all they know, to start working for a civilian company where they are surrounded by strangers, away from their military friends for the first time in many years.

During my first four years in business it was a very steep learning curve, especially as I had not prepared for or planned things in advance. Several mistakes were made, some having more impact than others. I am not sure if it was a case of leaving the army and reacting against all the rules and regulations I'd lived with over the years, but I went to the opposite extreme, following no rules and obeying nothing, rebelling against everything that I came across.

As it turns out, this is a very normal occurrence for someone who leaves the military after serving so long – 14 years in my case. You either remain regimented and rigid or you become the total opposite.

Through all the problems, the double-crossing, back-stabbing and of course my mistakes and negative actions which created many of the situations, I had no intention of hurting anybody. I never wished ill on anyone and always tried to rectify things that had gone wrong.

The ability to carry on when you are at the lowest point and it seems there is no way out, when you are scared of where you are and frightened to death of what is round the corner or of what might go wrong next, yet you still carry on – that is courage. There were times, when I was at my lowest ever point, that hearing the phone ring or the sound of an email notification made me feel physically sick. I couldn't answer the phone because I was so scared.

The feeling of worthlessness, loneliness, the inability to control or secure a way out of a truly crap situation, to the point where I wondered if life was worth carrying on, are things I will never shake or truly ever forget completely. They will haunt me forever.

However, somehow, something gave me heart. I believe courage played a huge part in my coming out the other side. Through all the bad times, when life is really testing every ounce of your being, if you can still do the right thing and carry on regardless – using each element of CDRILS, but most importantly having the courage to do the right thing – then you will be respected. You will earn a reputation as not only a courageous businessman, one who can keep their head held high, but also a courageous human being with the ability to do the right thing, simply because, it is the right thing to do.

This belief helped me to make two of the largest decision I think that I have had to make for many many years, certainly the largest decisions of my business career.

When I left the Army in 2012, the initial few months were exciting, nerve wrecking and very disorientating, I felt like I was on a long course which would end soon enough and I would be back to the Unit, back amongst my family. As time went on though, it became clear as the reality of it all sunk in, that this truly was the end and then the insecurities started hitting home. I suddenly had nothing, I had lost my family, my support network, my friends, my job security and my wage, what the hell was I going to do?

There really are no words that could possibly describe that feeling. I mean I had lived on the streets at points when I was younger, I had overdosed and been by myself in a bad place but even that does not come close to this! It was at this point when I started to remember certain images and fragments of memories, incidents, situations, but it was all jumbled up. I can look back now and identify at what point certain things started to happen and understand why I might have done what I did or maybe why I acted the way I did, however at the time…………..you just aren't ready to think about it.

The easy way I found to get by, was to throw myself into work, maybe this is why I didn't do any of the relevant planning that I should have done? I had to be physically busy every day and so I would ensure that I was running around doing something, anything, every day, seven days a week. On the one hand this meant that I was getting so much work done, I was networking, running the business, driving, writing marketing content, doing my own social media, meeting clients and thinking up new ideas. However on the other hand, I was working 16hr days plus, seven days a week, spinning so many plates, having no self-discipline, self-respect, no social life, wasn't eating well and started becoming stressed.

It was October 2015 when my then partner finally convinced me to go to the Drs and talk to them about stress. I was concerned over what I would be told, although never thought that it would be that bad, but knew they would want me to cut down on the number of hours I was working. It was then that PTSD first got brought up by a medical professional. When I told my partner……….well they weren't my partner anymore, lets just say that. So I ignored it again, until the company was hit with huge financial problems over the Christmas period, including a £10k mechanical bill for blown turbo's on the Jaguar chauffeur cars. This hit me hard, on top of my partner leaving and I just could not handle anymore, I crumbled, I was distraught, an emotional wreck and had been here once before many years ago when I had failed, but I didn't want to fail this time. The one thing, the only thing, that I could hold onto was/is my daughters and the thought of winning them back, seeing them again and so I gathered all the courage I could and rang Combat Stress. In February 2016 I was officially diagnosed with moderate to severe Post Traumatic Stress Disorder and in July 2016 I went to Combat Stress for two weeks' rehabilitation, which was my first big step forward along my PTSD journey.

Whilst I was there I turned 40 years old. Happy Birthday to me! It was at this point, whilst talking to my Key Worker, that the decision was made to change my name, move out of the hotel room I had been living in all year and confront the financial problems with the company. It was a huge decision that led to my having to make what felt like an impossible choice. I could either choose voluntary insolvency and walk away with financial security for me and my children, nice car and nice house but there would be thousands of pounds owed to colleagues, local businesses and suppliers that I had worked with for the past three years OR I could choose to stay and fight, try to work things out, use the finances to settle everything I could, then walk away. Find out what I did later in the book!!

Towards the end of 2016, I somehow managed to summon the courage to move, not just from the hotel, but away from Oxfordshire too and found a house to myself, in Buckingham. I once again found myself in a whole new region where no one knew me, with no support, little identity with my new surname and on the face of it, no new career.

I won't lie to you it was another very scary period in my life, one that I found a tremendous struggle and to be honest, initially I became more of a recluse for a period of time and I felt like I had failed my children.

This made me think about the transition I had been through, the journey I had travelled, to get to this juncture in my life and all the experience I had actually gained. I did not want others to feel like they had to make some of the decisions I did and so digging deep, I once more managed to find the courage from somewhere. I carried out due diligence, drew up a business plan, this time, gained a business coach and relaunched myself as a Military Transition Consultant and Life Coach.

Now I assist organisations in understanding, identifying and relating transferable military skills to their specific industry, to then further develop and deliver, a Transition Into Employment – TIE business model and framework that I designed. This ultimately provides Veterans with the right level of support needed through their transition and the organization with a return on investment, whilst supporting Veterans and arguably, the UK's economy. Through life coaching, I can help Veterans create specific, realistic and timely goals, basing my coaching on my own experiences, meaning I can relate to any anxieties, concerns or confusion. It is my way of helping other Forces individuals through their own transitions, providing one-to-one personal support during a period where I certainly wish I had had someone there whom I could rely on and who really understood what I was going through.

You see, personal life has a direct impact on your business life and if you are not happy at home, then you won't be happy in your work and this will most definitely have a negative impact to the detriment of you, your colleagues, your employer or your business. Courage therefore has many guises and affects every part of your life, as well as all those around you. Having the courage to do what is right, can and will change lives. I had the courage to make those hard decisions and to stand by them when I was questioning my own judgement. Even though I didn't have the belief in myself at times, I had the courage to carry on when the going was incredibly difficult and to reach out towards the ultimate goal. I completed the mission successfully, with my head held high.

What does Courage mean to you?

# Discipline

**Oxford Dictionary Definition** - *The practice of training people to obey rules or a code of behavior, using punishment to correct disobedience.*

**Operational Definition** - *Discipline is the primary antidote to fear and maintains operational effectiveness: it is supported by team loyalty, trust and professionalism. Discipline instils self-confidence and self-control. Good discipline means soldiers will do the right thing even under the most difficult of circumstances. This highlights the importance of Self-Discipline: Innate, not imposed, with the Army expecting self-discipline from every Soldier, and training aims to strengthen this.*

We all understand the requirement for discipline, across all walks of life, and I am sure we all have our own thoughts on what is classed as someone being a soft or harsh disciplinarian, dependent on the environment and/or situation. There is a specific necessity for discipline in the military, though, one which is backed by the harsh reality that if you lack discipline on the battlefield, then you, or worse, a colleague, could get seriously wounded or die.

Now thankfully this is not the case in business; however that does not mean you should merely pay lip service to this particular value. If you do, it could very easily destroy you and ruin your business. An overreaction on my part, surely?

Discipline in business presents itself in a variety of guises, so let's move on past the standard, basic things such as getting washed in the morning or doing as you're told by the boss. Those are a given, hopefully. If not, then feel free to reach out to me and I will happily arrange a "One-on-one" coaching session or day's workshop!

When Service leavers leave the fold, they tend to go one of two ways. They either A) remain regimented, highly disciplined and very military-like or B) they go the opposite way, becoming despondent, undisciplined and almost rebellious. If you're in this position, you have probably already identified which one of these two applies to you. If you are A, then you are probably thinking that this is the best one to be in business. But is it? There are pros and cons to both. Yes, A would appear to be more beneficial, however the problem with A is that it is possible to become so regimented that there is little or no flexibility. You can become very frustrated with others quickly, mainly because they are not performing as they should or lack communication.

The great thing with B is, it allows flexibility and flexibility in business is crucial. Not everything outside of the military is done in the same regimented way, people do not act as they should and you need to think outside of the box in order to achieve goals, specific outcomes or financial targets.

Prospective clients in business are in some ways similar to that of the enemy on a battlefield. You learn about the client, gain intelligence on their strengths and weaknesses, their characteristics, flaws, what motivates them and ultimately what are their specific requirements and aims. Once you have gained all the intelligence you can, you then draw up a plan of action, putting together a proposal as well as a selection of other plans, in case the client should change their requirements suddenly.

Just like any battle, no plan survives first contact and therefore the ability to think outside of the box, remaining flexible to clients' needs, is of paramount importance in order to secure the deal, or win the battle. Why go straight up the middle just because everyone else does? Be imaginative and flank them unexpectedly.

What has this to do with discipline? It takes discipline to put together all of the information, to start putting a plan together, to formulate the plan, make the necessary arrangements, planning and organising of requirements, and then to execute your plan; to not rush things, to collate only relevant information, to pay attention to detail and ensure every contingency is thought of. Having discipline and remaining disciplined throughout is a value that will be at the very heart of everything you do.

When liaising with clients you will require discipline on a number of levels, from biting your lip when you have a particularly difficult one, to remaining professional at all times, not flirting (or worse) with a good-looking client! When it comes to agreeing terms, securing a deal and competing with competitors, the amount of discipline that is required to not cross boundaries, overstep the mark and/or knowingly "turn" on associates/colleagues, simply to get that signed contract, can at times be truly overwhelming.

When I had the chauffeur company, I worked with several other similar chauffeur companies of various sizes, from small "one man bands" to large, global businesses. It is simply a factor of logistics that no chauffeur company can always have enough cars to meet every booking that comes though; it is always prudent to have trusted relationships with others in the same industry that you can call on.

At times I drove other companies' clients and they drove mine, an area of great concern for some – and rightly so, as you are competitors at the end of the day. What stops them from stealing your clients or you theirs? "Business is business" after all. This is, of course, where discipline comes into play once again.

Imagine yourself as a start-up chauffeur company, struggling to gain clients and needing money to pay for all those outgoings, when you get a booking from an associate at a huge chauffeur company to drive their top client whose account is worth fifty thousand pounds a year. You collect the client, get on really well with them, they are very impressed by you and make a comment about it being good if you could drive them again. What do you do? Do you give them your business card? Do you say sorry but he would need to go through the other chauffeur company? Aside from all the other values and standards that are brought into question in this scenario, ultimately it is the discipline you have within yourself that dictates whether or not you stand by your beliefs, values and standards or risk it all, chasing the money, but by doing so potentially destroying your reputation and ruining your business.

I have been in this very situation at several points in time over the years, some when I was at my lowest, cash flow was pretty much non-existent and I was literally clinging on to the business with all my might. I was watching the pennies, let alone the pounds. One such point was over the Royal Ascot weekend. To chauffeur companies, such sporting occasions can be worth a lot of money, should you be driving the right kind of clientele. This particular weekend I was. The tasking was a simple case of collecting from London, driving to Royal Ascot, then waiting around all day until they were ready to go and driving them home; each day for three days.

The couple owned a successful company and we got on very well – extremely well – and they talked to me about all kinds of personal things. On the last day, when everyone gets even more drunk than the other days, we were on the drive home late at night when they offered me a job driving for them personally. The role involved a huge wage and various perks of the job: accommodation, clothing allowance for suits, using the car when they weren't. They were going to stop using the chauffeur company who gave me this tasking and employ me full time instead. I said no. What would you do?

I had earned a great deal of money from the company who provided me with the task and they would send me more in the future; then there was the bigger picture of how it would seem to others, taking someone's client from under them when they had trusted me with driving them. The trust and respect they had shown me in providing me with that job and others was such that I simply could not go against them and abuse that trust.

The bigger picture, of that company, my associates, trusting and respecting me as a person, as a professional and as a businessman, meant more to me than the money; but trust me, it took all my discipline to not accept.

At the other end of the scale – and something that Service leavers are well known for overlooking – is that you have the everyday discipline of those in the military. Turning up for "Parade" five minutes before the five minutes, working alongside those you respect and trust but do not get on with, following orders to the best of your ability in a professional manner even if the task is a particularly distasteful or boring one.

These are examples of situations that require you to be disciplined and as such, they are useful to illustrate discipline to potential employers. How many civilians would sweep leaves outside, on a windy autumn's day, for no apparent reason other than you were ordered to do so?

This takes respect for the rank (although obviously not for the person at that moment in time), respect for the rules of the Service, corp, unit and ultimately, discipline.

Employers recognise and respect the discipline of the Armed Forces individual; however they can be slightly wary of it too. They can see it as being very "regimented" and inflexible, so it is imperative that you are also able to demonstrate your ability to be flexible. Flexibility is another key skill and one that will continue to aid you in everything you do.

What does Discipline mean to you?

# Respect

**Oxford Dictionary Definition -** *A feeling of deep admiration for someone or something elicited by their abilities, qualities, or achievements.*

**Operational Definition -** *Respect for others, both those inside and outside of our organisation is not only a legal obligation, it is a fundamental principle of the freedom that our society enjoys. Teams that embrace diversity, and value each individual for their contribution and viewpoint are always stronger for it. We must treat everyone we encounter, as we would wish to be treated.*

Respect for others comes from the duty to put others first. It means that there is no place for prejudice or favoritism. Like loyalty, respect for others goes both up and down the chain of command and sideways amongst peers. The Army's recruiting motto and long-standing ethos: 'Be the Best', can only have true meaning if everyone it includes not merely benefits from equality of treatment and opportunity, but also believes in, upholds and lives by this in everything they do.

This rightly extends to the treatment of all human beings,

especially the victims of conflict, the dead, the wounded, prisoners and civilians, particularly those we have deployed to help. All soldiers must act within the law and the very nature of complex, modern day operations makes it essential that they maintain the highest standards of decency, fairness and respect at all times, even under the most difficult of conditions.

However, we are not talking about the Army or the Armed Forces here. We are not talking about soldiers anymore but civvies in a civvie world, working within civvie businesses. So how does talking about respect within the Armed Forces and in areas of conflict relate to business? Isn't it a bit extreme? The straight answer is, "Yes, it is"; however we are talking about military skills in business, the importance and value of these to you as an employer, employee and/or self-employed businessman; and also about improving your understanding of the military mind.

To truly understand this, you need to know the lengths that the military will go to to uphold these skills, beliefs, values and standards. Could you still respect a person after they have just blown up, shot, killed, maimed or injured your best friend, and then go about your job in a professional manner?

Whilst I am sure that most will think they know and understand the meaning of respect, do you truly employ it within your life, to its fullest extent? This is an area that was a great challenge for me. After spending 14 years in a world where you lived and breathed this value and upheld it regardless of what was going on in your life or around you, where you still respected someone even if you did not like them or agree with their thoughts or beliefs, to one where people talk down to you for no reason and act out so disrespectfully, or so it seemed to me, was extremely frustrating.

I did not make it up to the dizzying heights of a Warrant Officer or make commissioning; however I have friends and colleagues who have. They informed me of how difficult a transition it can be, to find themselves as an employee where a young team leader or line manager, with little training or life experience, was talking down to them and failing to identify or utilise their skills, training and experience. You could argue that this is not the line manager's or young team leader's fault, it is simply a case of a lack of leadership and management training. To a point I would agree, and this is where organisations could benefit from identifying from the very beginning of employment the skills a veteran holds. However, is it not also the responsibility of that individual and quite simply down to their shortsightedness and lack of respect for their subordinates? To be very clear with you I believe, yes, indeed it is!

There is, moreover, more to this value than merely the word respect. You also have: respect for others, respect for your organisation, its values, its ethos, its rules, your superiors and respect for yourself. There are countless connotations to the value respect.

Integration with a work force of any size is always going to be a key area of concern for any Service leaver, veteran or employer and this will quite simply boil down to respect on both sides. There has always been and always will be a certain divide or "us and them" mentality within areas of both the military and civilian populations. I am not going to enter into a debate here, as it's a large topic; all I will say is that apart from the fact that we are all individuals, the difference of mindset between typical civilians and Service people comes back to the fact that in hostile situations, respect has the ability to save lives.

To build rapport with another person, you first need to understand them: what makes them who they are, why they act or think the way they do. We then decide whether we feel a connection or can relate to this – if not we walk away, if we do, then we build a relationship.

Within the context of work, you do not have the same freedom to walk away, so you need to come to a mutual understanding: "Ok, so we do not like each other, however we need to work together, so let's just get on with our jobs and be civil". You learn to respect one another and act professionally. That's the ideal; but we all know that life is not always so straightforward. Unfortunately, within the context of "civilian and military", in some cases a prejudgment has already been made about the other person: how they might act, how they might think and how they might be. This can happen on both sides.

People might be defensive, walls might be built and barriers put in place, before the veteran has even started work. In most cases this is not too much of a problem, more of an adjustment. It could quite as easily happen with a new civilian starting work; it is merely an area to be mindful of.

Integration is an important factor when taking on any new employees. For companies employing a number of ex-Service personnel, it is useful to have a "military transition programme" in place, covering the interview and induction process as well. There is a specific model for training available to assist with this, which more and more organisations – although currently mainly larger PLCs – are using.

Where this issue does arise, I recommend you see it as a challenge. We all need a challenge of some kind in our lives, to make us feel alive – although we might moan about it, and veterans are great at moaning about life!

In my case, though, whilst running the business over these past few years, this has been a difficult area for me. I expected those who I worked alongside, associated with, networked with and carried out business with, to act in the same manner and uphold the same values as those who I lived, breathed and fought alongside in the military.

When this wasn't the case, I sometimes got extremely frustrated. I was disappointed and hurt. I simply could not understand why people were acting, in my mind, so cruelly. I took everything very personally. This was compounded by PTSD; I accept that this is one of my "Challenges" to overcome and not anyone else's problem, but I could physically feel the lack of respect from various individuals and it was draining.

The first step to adjusting is, "Accept" that things are going to be different. This is probably what those who have not experienced a lack of respect have subconsciously already done prior to leaving the military. This is a "Key" area, something you really must get to grips with in order to smooth your transition. Accept that things are going to be different; accept that you are going to have to start from the bottom again and work your way up; accept that people might have preconceptions of you and have barriers up against you; accept that people might not think the same or work at the same intensity as in the military; and accept that you will face several difficult challenges along your journey – and it is a journey, your transition will not happen overnight!

Respect is earned, not bought or immediately given. You could say that you have earned respect for time served in the military and for the most part you will receive this respect. However, this does not earn you "Carte-Blanche" within the work place or in business, to do what you want. Once you have reached the three or four year point as a veteran, you will find that your time served will begin to mean less to some. I have personally seen people's reactions change. When I said that I had been out only one or two years they were excited, interested and respectful; now when I say that I have been out four years they seem less respectful of the fact that I have served. Now it is more of a case of, I am not in the Army anymore, so get on with it…

It has taken all my courage, discipline and integrity to carry on, to build a successful business regardless, to face and overcome the challenges that life threw at me along the way. Through it all, I have done my utmost to continue to respect everyone I came across, regardless of what they may or may not have done to me, regardless as to their thoughts, preconceptions or opinions of me.

I do not want a medal for it, I've got enough of those to clean. I would just like for people to try and understand one another, when they meet someone get to know them first: who they are, what they are about; and at the very least respect them as another human being.

Hang on, what about "self-respect" I hear you cry and yes you are absolutely right, this is indeed an area that must not go unmentioned or in the case of yourselves, simply cast to one side.

Just like you cannot expect people to love you, if you do not love yourself, how could you possibly complain about people disrespecting you, if you do not have any respect for yourself to begin with. Look at yourself in the mirror and ask whether you could honestly respect the person who stands before you? Now this only works if you can be brutally honest, it is a very slippery slope if you start the waking day, by kidding yourself!

I personally place self-respect alongside self-belief and self-discipline. If you do not believe in yourself, respect one self, and have the self-discipline to uphold these values and instill them all the time, for you, no one else. Then you will find that every day will be an uphill battle for you personally, let alone how it will impact on your professional image.

I know all of this is so easy to say, however out in the real world, it can be a totally different animal, especially when there are so many who hold such blatant disregard for anyone, aside from themselves. However, regardless of what happens, remain true to yourself, follow your personal beliefs, stand by your values and continue with your high standards. Then people will want to know you, work with you, do business with you, be your client and ultimately ……. respect you as you respect yourself.

What does Respect mean to you?

# Integrity

**Oxford Dictionary Definition -** *The quality of being honest and having strong moral principles.*

**Operational Definition -** *Integrity means being truthful and honest, which develops trust amongst individuals and welds them into robust and effective teams. Integrity is therefore critical to soldiering, as soldiers must have complete trust in one and other as their lives might ultimately depend on it. Trust in the Chain of Command is also key, and demands integrity from those in positions of authority.*

I personally hold this value in very high esteem and would like to say that throughout my life – although not so much when I was a youth – I have always been thought of as an individual with integrity and strong moral principles. It could be argued that as a man of principles these have, at times, caused friction within certain relationships. This is where I have learned two key skills in life - accountability and flexibility.

Integrity in business though, is there really any? Looking at both definitions, being truthful, honest and having strong moral principles – can any businessman say that they wholly uphold this value, to the true meaning of its definition?

Do not get me wrong, I am sure that there are a number of business individuals out there who are genuine and have undeniable values, of which integrity is only one. My comment may seem like a huge generalisation where I am tarring everybody with the same brush. However, the Armed Forces as an institution, wholeheartedly promotes its values and standards. It is drummed into its Soldiers Under Training (SUTs) or Recruits, during Phase 1 training – I know as I was an Instructor for two years – whereas, out in "Civvie Street", it is not a requirement and few outside of those who raised you will instill the importance of beliefs, values and standards.

It therefore becomes a choice, which then collides with the main of purpose of being in business, the main reason behind the insecurities of so many and the main thing that can destroy a person's values at the click of the fingers: money.

Being in business will test every value that you hold dear, it will test who you are as a person and the lengths you will go to in order to make a success of what you set out to do, the achievements you intend to reach. The level of testing I would not have thought possible and I still find it a little hard to believe even now. After all, I served 14 years and successfully completed several Operational Tours to some of the most inhospitable places in the world, facing some of the most terrifying and horrendous situations. Surely I could handle basic business?

The problem is that whilst the military may operate in very similar ways to that of a business, the one very important factor we do not have to concern us is money. The decisions we make in the military, for the most part, are not affected by money. Although in worst-case scenarios we may have to make decisions that could save or take away someone's life, those decisions are not based around money.

The purpose of any business is to make money. Everything else that follows – and the outcomes of a successful business: economy, employment, infrastructure, communities, well-being, families – these are all secondary. Although in business worst-case scenario decisions will not impact on the life or death of someone, however, they can affect someone's promotion, employment, cause loss of a client, loss of business or even having to close a business, which in turn will have serious repercussions whereby people lose their livelihood, families and homes.

Everyday decisions are made that will have repercussions for someone else in business, somewhere in the world and every decision you make will in some way, shape or form, cost someone money. THIS is why I posed the question earlier: *"Integrity in business though, is there really any? Looking at both definitions, being truthful, honest and having strong moral principles – can any businessman say that they wholly uphold this value, to the true meaning of its definition?"*

It is not a case of my questioning any specific individual and how they were prior to being in business or even who they are whilst in business, it is more a case of their ability to make the right decisions, based upon their beliefs, values and standards. Have they the courage – both physical and moral courage – to remain integral, by being truthful and honest, whilst those around them make decisions based solely upon money?

Now that has opened a can of worms. I can almost hear people throwing this book down in disgust and see images of some very red faces, with steam piping out of their ears! I am not here to judge, none of us are angels and many have at some point or other crossed the line in some way. There are also many decisions that simply have to be made in life, that go against our values. The ability to carry out every task in life with integrity, unfortunately, just cannot be achieved. Sometimes life ……… just happens.

I was, and in many ways still am, very naïve when I first came into business. I had the thought process I mentioned before: that after everything I had seen, I could handle being in business. I wanted to bring all the values – and most of all integrity – into business. My company was going to stand for truth, honesty and strong moral principles. I was going to use this as my key USP – Unique Selling Point – as I thought it would seem like a breath of fresh air to prospective clients, and would attract them to do business with me.

I was amazed at how poor the levels of customer service were, in general within any industry. Obviously some companies are better than others, however on the whole, customer service really is pretty rubbish. Think of yourself as a client, what would you like from a supplier? A good product and/or the right service, of course; but also wouldn't you simply want the people you deal with to be upfront, honest and trustworthy? Basically, you want them to have Integrity!

On the face of it, having integrity should not be a problem. We have already said that as clients we want integrity from our providers, we want them to be truthful and honest. The problem is, though, that if you are too honest in business then someone may take advantage of this, use it against you or beat you to a prospective client and win the contract. If you trust others too much, there will be those who will use this to their advantage, befriend you, gain what they need and then use it against you, go over your head, speak untruths about you, and take business from you. It is wise to be careful whom you trust.

Then there are those situations you face in business that will test your own integrity to the limit. I am ashamed to say that at times, I did not manage to uphold all of my values and integrity was one of them. I told the story earlier: money was tight, I had made bad decisions, had large invoices to pay, then I was defrauded of one of my chauffeur cars. It was a defining moment for me, one which saw me finally going in for two weeks PTSD rehabilitation.

In the following months I somehow managed to find the strength to claw myself back from despair, but I knew the challenges I faced ahead were great. I began by regaining my integrity, accepting responsibility for my actions, having the flexibility to think outside of the box and with grim determination, fought for my values, my dignity and eventually my self-belief.

It worked. It had its challenges and many an adjustment was needed along the way, however as a company we earned respect and a reputation for being a reliable, professional and trustworthy business. This was echoed by our clients, who remained loyal to us when many others came knocking on their door, promising bigger and better deals, but they did not leave us because I cared, I was honest and I respected them each as individuals.

Integrity has a unique significance to soldiering. It is essential for there to be trust in one another. As is mentioned at the beginning of the chapter, "their lives might ultimately depend on it"; yet of course in business there are no such dire outcomes should there be a lack of integrity, honesty and trust. However, as all forms of deceit and dishonesty constitute a lack of integrity, calling into question whether an individual can be relied upon, this can ultimately damage any team and its operational effectiveness, regardless as to the *battlefield*.

There is in business an actual necessity for an element of trust and honesty, because people buy from people. This being the case, without a certain amount of trust and honesty from both parties involved, no business relationship would evolve – to the detriment of both – and this is true regardless of whether you are employed or self-employed.

What does Integrity mean to you?

# Loyalty

**Oxford Dictionary Definition -** *The quality of being loyal (Giving or showing firm and constant support or allegiance to a person or institution). A strong feeling of support or allegiance.*

**Operational Definition -** *Loyalty binds all ranks of the Army together, creating cohesive teams that can achieve far more than the sum of their parts. The Nation, Army and Chain of Command rely on the continuing allegiance, commitment and support of all who serve. But, loyalty is not blind and must operate within the parameters of the other Values; it should not stop appropriate action to prevent transgressions by subordinates, peers or seniors.*

Loyalty binds all ranks of the Army together: it goes both up and down. It turns individuals into teams, creating and strengthening the formations, units and sub-units of which the Army is composed. The Nation, the Army and the chain of command rely on the continuing allegiance, commitment and support of all who serve: that is, on their loyalty. Equally important is that all soldiers, and their families, must be confident that the Army and the Nation will treat them with loyalty and fairness. The Army's loyalty to the individual is expressed in the Military Covenant – it manifests itself in justice, fair rewards, and life-long support to all soldiers.

Those in authority must be loyal to their subordinates: representing their interests faithfully, dealing with complaints thoroughly and developing their abilities through progressive training. Subordinates must be loyal to their leaders, their team, and their duty. Being loyal to one's leaders or subordinates does not mean that wrong-doing should be condoned or covered up: this is misplaced loyalty and damages a soldier's integrity. Loyalty, though expected, must be earned through commitment, self-sacrifice, courage, professionalism, decency and integrity. These qualities are required both on and off duty as they are enduring characteristics that cannot be turned on and off at will.

Anyone who has served even minimal time within the Forces has experienced the strength gained by serving amongst those who are loyal. After all, in battle, it is this loyalty that binds us, provides greater strength and allows us to carry on whilst enduring hardships, to see this through and fulfil our tasks successfully.

That is battle, however, and we are talking about business – surely these are two very different subjects? No! The title of this book is *The Business Battlefield*; the two subjects are very similar. Although thankfully there are no bullets, bombs and/or insurgents to physically hurt us, there are many other different ways we can be hurt, mentally and emotionally, if we are not careful.

From my personal experience, loyalty in business is something that is considerably lacking; after integrity it is the value I hold in highest esteem.

If you have little courage, are not very disciplined or respectful, but have unquestionable integrity and loyalty, then I would still have you work for me. Obviously if I had the choice between that person and one who holds more values, then I would go for the other; but I believe that should someone have integrity and loyalty and little else, then that might just be enough.

The other values without integrity and loyalty will not be enough. You can have a businessman who is very kind, smooth, polite, disciplined and respectful, but who then has the courage to go behind your back and double cross you to land a deal or steal a client away from you.

If they had integrity and loyalty to you, they would not carry out such actions and would instead support you, pass on the deal or simply decline the client.

You might say, "Business is business at the end of the day" and it is a "Dog-eat-dog world", so we must do what we need to in order to survive. I don't agree. Yes it is business, yes it is very difficult out there and yes, there will always be others who would happily do that to you, however, YOU have a strong set of beliefs, values and standards, whereby you have the courage and discipline to not simply follow the sheep and do as others do. You respect other human beings and the feelings they have, you have integrity and loyalty, and you act in a way that demonstrates this, turning your back on those who act without them. Your business is always conducted with this set of beliefs, values and standards at the very heart of all that you do.

This in turn earns you the respect of others within your industry and the wider business fraternity. It will also gain you a reputation for being a fair and respectable businessman, one who people will want to work with and clients will want to give their money to. People buy from people.

In the previous example of the businessman going behind your back to land the deal or steal the client, should they be successful then it would only be a matter of time for their real personality to shine through, and should the client realise what they are doing then they are very likely to turn them down. Should you be the businessman who passes on a deal because your colleague was there first and you show this support in front of the client, both will respect you all the more for it and recommend you to others down the line, simply because of your beliefs, values and standards. You had the courage to turn business down, you had the respect, whilst demonstrating integrity and loyalty for your colleague. By doing this you may have lost out financially in the short term, however in the bigger picture, you have gained significantly.

I found it very easy initially in business. I had already lived by my own beliefs and the Army's values and standards for many years. They saw me safe through several Operational Tours and many a situation, although I was tested many a time, along with these values, and I questioned them on more than a couple of occasions. However, I came out the other side and with very few "Battle Scars" compared to others, so believed I simply needed to carry this on and stand by them through my new venture and my new life.

What I failed to do though, was to take into consideration one overriding factor in business that affects decisions and creates challenges at every single turn and every step you take: other people! Whilst I was fully trusting and laying my life out in front of others, laying myself bare for all to see, those around me saw a huge opportunity to take advantage of this, of me, of my situation and my weaknesses, which they grabbed with both hands. By God they started to twist, steal, scheme and plot ways in which they could benefit. And me? What about me? ......... I should not have been so trusting!

People in business are a very different breed, just like those in the Forces are compared to civilians. I unfortunately assumed that I could simply trust everyone, as I did in the Army, and everyone would be the same, act the same and behave the same way. It took a while before the full extent of how my being so trusting evolved and came back to bite me in the arse – and when it did, everything seemed to come at once, from every angle, leaving me questioning absolutely everything, especially myself.

This has happened on several occasions over the years, to the point where a true friend of mine, my first "Civvie Friend", turned to me towards the end of 2016 and said: "What is it exactly about you that makes people want to stab you in the back?"; to which I simply replied: "I really don't know, I guess I am just too honest and naïve".


What does Loyalty mean to you?

# Selfless Commitment

**Oxford Dictionary Definition -** *Concerned more with the needs and wishes of others than with one's own.*

**Operational Definition -** *Selfless commitment is a foundation of military service, soldiers must be prepared to serve where and when required and always give their best. The needs of the mission and the team come before personal interests. Ultimately, soldiers may be required to give their lives for their country, that is true selfless commitment.*

"I Nick Wilson, swear by Almighty God, that I will be faithful and bear true allegiance to Her Majesty Queen Elizabeth II, her heirs and successors and that I will as in duty bound honestly and faithfully defend her Majesty, her heirs and successors in person, crown and dignity, against all enemies and will observe and obey all orders of Her Majesty, her heirs and successors and of the generals and officers set over me."

Those who do not believe in God replace *"swear by almighty God"* with *"solemnly, sincerely and truly declare and affirm"*.

Irrespective of private beliefs, this oath embodies the context within which the British Army fights and operates. It expresses the loyalty of every soldier to the Sovereign as Head of State. These relationships find expression in the Colors, Standards and the emblems of Regimental and Corps spirit, which derive from the Sovereign. Personal commitment is the foundation of military service.

For me this has been one of the hardest chapters to write, aside from the obvious demonstrations of such a value within a military context, putting the needs of others above your own in training and on the battlefield, ensuring you protect those around you and the weaker members of your team. To then translate this to a business battlefield scenario, where there are different dangers around and more importantly a whole new mindset in people, is indeed a challenge. It is one of the rarest values you could possibly come across and whilst I hold integrity in such high esteem, true selfless commitment, when demonstrated wholly, has to be the most powerful value as it is one that goes against our natural instincts as human beings, of self-preservation.

I carried out a lot of charity work during my time in the military, from putting together dinner auction events, arranging the 1st Basrah Valentines Half Marathon – with over 450 multi-national military and civilian personnel participating – or planning the 1000 mile non-stop cycle through Europe for the 60th anniversary of D-Day. I guess you could say that I like to do my part and help others, something that has seen those who have taken part and supported me over the years raise some £50,000. For that I personally offer a huge thank you to everyone.

Within a business context though, this would be known as

Corporate Social Responsibility – CSR – whereby you carry out work within the community, support local services and other local businesses. Clients also nowadays like to see that the company they have a working relationship with demonstrates some type of CSR and/or supports charities. They may even be more inclined to choose a company who carries out CSR, supports local businesses and charities, which would in turn demonstrate the values of selfless commitment, against those who do not.

People buy from people and with loyalty and selfless commitment being the rarest values nowadays, if you can demonstrate these in a positive manner, the implication and affects these can have amongst those around you will stand you out amongst the crowd. If you go self-employed this would be seen as a Unique Selling Point – USP – as are all the values we have been discussing.

Supporting fellow small businesses in the same industry and those around you – be it competitors or suppliers – understanding their own challenges and finding ways to help them – if you are willing to do this then people will respect you. Your reputation for having such a highly regarded value and the work you do for others, putting their needs and requirements above your own, will be noticed, valued and ultimately respected by your colleagues, your peers and, more importantly, your clients and prospective clients.

By demonstrating this as an employee, you will find yourself earning promotion, climbing your way progressively up the professional ladder, so to speak. This value is easy to understand and identify with, however it is one of the hardest values to demonstrate within the business and corporate context.

Charity work is an easy way of demonstrating selfless commitment, but one that does not show it in a real-time business context.

Earlier in the book, I spoke about my being officially diagnosed with PTSD and struggling with financial difficulties, well I pick up where I had a £10k mechanical bill from before Christmas. It is May 2016 and I have now also, just been defrauded out of one of my Jaguar chauffeur cars, which saw me losing out on over £8k in payments, right at the point where we were busier than ever and cashflow was key.

I was still unsure how I was going to cope with the loss of one of the cars, when it came the time for the other car to be handed back, leaving me with nothing (apart from a headache!) Bookings were still on the increase. There was talk from a couple of contacts regarding a possible investment, but nothing was forthcoming past the verbal meetings. That experience taught me to not get excited about anything until contracts are signed and funds have been transferred. I had effectively become a booking agent. I had negotiated a basic commission rate with another car company, that was to play a much larger role in the company further down the line, so things were settling down a bit.

All the work had to be subbed (issued), out to other chauffeur companies in order to keep my clients. I had no spare money, due to my credit rating, I couldn't get any loans, funding or even an overdraft from the bank. Times were desperate, complicated and frustrating. We were busier than we had ever been, turning over £22k pm and yet I could not secure any financial support to enable the company to grow in line with the increase of clients. The debts were piling up and suppliers were getting frustrated with me, and rightly so.

I met with my accountants and we discussed voluntary insolvency. That would solve my problems financially, but it would mean my independent suppliers would be left without payment and some clients would be left short – including brides-to-be who had booked wedding cars. After a long discussion, several days with little sleep and speaking with those few individuals around me I trusted, I made the decision to not take the insolvency, but to face the music instead, working my way through things until everything was paid and everyone was looked after. I didn't want to leave anyone out of pocket, regardless of what it meant to me and how it might affect me. You can say that this decision took courage, by the very definition of the word – "ability to do something that frightens one" – and trust me when I say that I was frightened. In fact I wasn't merely frightened, I was "bricking it". I also believe that it brought in the other values too – discipline, respect, integrity, loyalty and selfless commitment – but mainly it took courage to not simply make the decision, but to actually stand by it.

With the work now being subbed out, I took this time to commit to attending rehabilitation with Combat Stress, so that I might be able to gain a better understanding of what the PTSD truly meant and how it was affecting me. It was obviously affecting my decision making and had ultimately contributed to my costing the company financially.

It was during this time that I came to the ultimate decision to negotiate a merger of my company with another, then sell the brand.

So I sold the company, started to make arrangements to pay those I owed money to and eventually managed to walk away with my head held high, debt free and so much wiser and richer, even if it was from experiences gained rather than financially.

Throughout this whole process I was guided by the very clear goal of paying off all that I owed and straightening out my life. I had become so engrossed within the business that I had lost all clarity of who I was, where my life was heading and any goals I may have had, apart from a vague desire to take over the world. In some ways I had become Del Boy. As corny as it sounds, I think we all become a bit like that character – otherwise why would we get into business in the first place? But there is a very fine line between working hard to build your business/empire and becoming too involved and too close to it. It's easy to get engulfed within it all; and this is not helped by the lack of support available, or the fact that external events impact your everyday running of a business and living your own life.

In life as well as business there are far too many people who tell you what they think you want to hear, or say all the good things to you, usually because they want something from you. A true friend is someone who tells you the harsh truths as well as the nice-to-hear stuff, is it not?

People often do not have the courage to tell you the truth or stay true to their word once they have committed to something. That was not going to be me.

Making the initial decision to stay, sorting out as much as I could personally, paying out of my own disability benefits and going without a wage. It was a very scary, emotional and upsetting period, which saw me putting the needs of these suppliers above my own. I worked so hard to see this through. I felt like a failure, wondered what had it all been for and what I had to show for it. To then make the following decision and sell the company, using the money to clear the outstanding debts, would leave nothing. There would be no financial security for my kids, no nice car, no nice house and no huge payout at the end.

However I could not see others struggling because of my own mistakes and whilst others can always question my business decisions, I would like to think that my values and standards, reputation and honor are beyond reproach. I walked away with my head held high.

Was it the right decision? I think it is one of personal opinion and whether you measure success by finances or happiness; it's a matter of where your beliefs, values and standards lie.

It would have been much easier for me had I chosen to go insolvent and merely walked away with the money. There would be less stress, upset and certainly emotionally it would have been much healthier for me to have taken the easy option of insolvency. However, I simply could not live with myself knowing that I had walked away from local small businesses like myself owing money when I could have paid them. These were not large companies who could afford to lose a few hundred or thousands of pounds and they were people I had built a trusting relationship with. Yes it took time and they were not happy about it – rightly so, I had let them down and I had to accept it was my fault, I had to accept responsibility for my actions.

For me though, it was the right decision and one that I would make again, although I would hope to not be in such a position again – after all, we should all learn from our mistakes!

What does Selfless Commitment mean to you?

# Summary

Since leaving the Army some four years ago now and having experienced the transition that every Service leaver must face – albeit my own personal version; each transition is personal to that individual – I have seen firsthand the challenges that must be overcome. The immediate problem for most will be employment, although for some housing is a more pressing issue, more so for those who look through rose-tinted glasses and think that their mum's brother's wife's son has a building company and will employ them at £1000 per week! You can go straight into a good job and some do, settling down straight away, enjoying their life and moving on with no problems; however unfortunately this kind of outcome is in the minority.

Secondary to employment is the transition itself, which might not show for three or four years. As mentioned above, for some it may not show at all, however everyone will have to overcome a varying number of challenges. To complicate things further, the transition itself can be broken down into several areas, transitioning into: Civvie Street, employment, life away from the military, relocation and relationships, not forgetting those who have injuries, regardless of whether they are mental or physical, they are one and the same, and certainly affect your life away from the military support.

That being said, the most important thing to remember is who you are, where you have come from, the training and experiences you have had, the strength you have shown in the face of all manner of adversities and how valuable all this is to the outside world. You need to remain strong, yet accept that things will be more different than maybe you realise; identify all those skills you have and relate them directly to the specific industry and company you apply for. Ensure you are happy with who you really are as a person, your beliefs, values and standards, then stand by them. Look for a company that holds similar values to your own, as this will be a great combat indicator for a good rapport and relationship between you both, which is vitally important.

Whilst there is much work being done to support Service leavers and veterans through the life transition and the transition into employment, there is still a great deal to be done. Many organisations continue to be unclear of how military skills transfer into their own specific industries and are wary of the stigma that is unjustly attached to the typical veteran, of having "Baggage" that would have a negative impact on the business.

There is a gap between the veteran and the employer, one which requires a leap of faith for some, whilst with others it will be more like a command task. Instead of rope, planks and oil drums, you have your experience, training, knowledge and military skills. It can be done, just carry out a thorough recce and detailed planning prior to moving forward.

For me, over the past four years I have transitioned from the military to civilian life, completed a transition into employment initially, before then moving into self-employment and starting my own business. Although I did eventually make a success of the chauffeur company before selling it on to another business, I was lucky – I thought that I could "Go with the flow" and didn't have that much of a plan. I did carry out my research and planning to a point, but it was certainly nowhere near the level it should have been.

Out of all the lessons learned, the importance of having structure and planning in place, whatever it is that you are doing or intend to do, is the most valuable. This is quite ironic when you think of it, after 14 years in the Army and with all the global fundraising events I have successfully arranged, you would have thought that structure and planning would have been my number one strength! I cannot explain this and believe me I have tried to think as to why it is the case. All I know is that I have hurt so many people along the way, destroyed relationships, been prevented from seeing my children and lost sight of my self-belief and values.

Although I was diagnosed with PTSD and that combined with my spinal injury meant I was eventually officially classed as being Disabled, I had to accept that these are simply additional challenges that must be overcome and can instead be used for good. This for me meant having the flexibility to adapt my skills so I could start assisting and guiding others along their own life paths and enhancing lives.

Acceptance and flexibility are two key words, ones that you will face time and again. It's not that you haven't faced them before during your service, however they might appear more intense out in Civvie Street.

Through all of this and through becoming a businessman, running a business and being an entrepreneur, I have done my utmost to remain true to my beliefs, values and standards, whilst utilising all of my military skills, training and experiences, in the most relevant manner. I did not always achieve this, I would lose sight of a number of these at times, and at others, I simply failed miserably, letting down my children, family, friends and supporters. We are all individuals, with a wide variety of skills, training and experiences, however as military personnel we have the unique advantage of having a whole host of exceptional additions to these. It is down to us to ensure that we highlight these in the correct manner, making sure they, and we, do not go unrecognised.

Am I a businessman in the true sense of the word then? No, I do not think I have what it takes to be a businessman as the world understands that term. I hold dear my personal beliefs, values and standards too much for me to make the calculated, difficult and at times harsh decisions required to ultimately make money. I see myself as an entrepreneur, an ideas guy who has the ability to look outside of the box and see things from varying perspectives, whilst identifying niche areas that others will miss. I am a "people person" and as such I rely on this to network, build rapport with possible valuable contacts, build relationships and sell myself – because as a Consultant and Life Coach, I am the product and people buy from people.

Business is all about the money and whilst military skills, beliefs, values and standards are, on the whole, invaluable in business, people will regard them in varying levels. If money can be saved by not implementing a few or all of these, then that is what some may do in order to increase their overall profits.

At the end of the day, business is all about making money and that is why we go into business. This is where self-belief, values and standards become confusing and at times extremely difficult, with very blurred lines, especially where money is concerned, and hard decisions – harsh, real-life, realistic decisions – have to be made in business, which can affect people's lives and families' livelihoods.

This is **"The Business Battlefield"**.

If you have enjoyed

*The Business Battlefield*

please post your review on Amazon and

connect with me on Facebook

facebook.com/wilsonslife

Visit my website www.wilsonslife.co.uk

Or email me at inspireme@wilsonslife.co.uk

With very great thanks,

Nick.

## About Nick

Nick Wilson is an ex-Serviceman who served 14 years in the British Army, including Operational Tours in Northern Ireland, Kosovo, Iraq and Afghanistan. Whilst not on Tour he assisted during the strikes of fire fighters, fuel tanker drivers and prison guards, and helped communities during the UK's worst floods.

An avid charity supporter and fundraiser, he has also arranged several large scale events to raise money, including a 1000 mile non-stop cycle ride from Esbjerg, Denmark to Ranville in France for the 60th Anniversary of D-Day and a half marathon, including multi coalition armed forces, around Basrah airport in Iraq, whilst deployed on Operations, to name but two.

As an entrepreneur post-Discharge, he set up his own chauffeur company, at the same time working to support other ex-Military personnel in making their transition to "Civvie Street".

Having been finally "officially" diagnosed with Post Traumatic Stress Disorder by Combat Stress in 2016, Nick has worked tirelessly to raise awareness of the struggle veterans and their families face on a daily basis. Together with a friend he set up Oxfordshire's first locally-based PTSD support group: "First Step Forward", which held it's first meeting in July 2016.

In January 2017, Nick was officially classed as Disabled, due to his PTSD, but also chronic spinal pain that he has been battling with since before his leaving the Army. He continues to face this challenge head on and utilizes his experiences of this, the bad and the good, to help signpost others and support where he can through First Step Forward.

Having personally experienced the adjustment to the harsh realities of business, he now works as a Military Transition Consultant, Life Coach and Speaker. As a Consultant he helps companies to understand how transferable military skills are into any industry, highlighting the skills possessed by military service leavers. As a Life Coach, he is assisting people to identify their own personal goals and gain life/work balance. Nick is also a qualified Neuro Linguistic Programming Practitioner and consults with companies over leadership and management development within the workplace, whilst also providing assistance to Service personnel and veterans with their transitions into civilian life and/or business.

Following his own deep beliefs, he is proud to demonstrate the values and standards of the Army: courage, discipline, respect, integrity, loyalty and selfless commitment.

In early February 2017, days prior to this book being sent for publishing, Nick signed the Armed Forces Covenant on behalf of his company Wilsons Life and two days later, was presented with a Bronze Award under the Employment Recognition Scheme, for his work and continued commitment to supporting the Armed Forces.